FOR ORGANS, PIANOS & ELECTRONIC KEYBOARDS

148

Italian Songs

ISBN 978-1-4234-0991-5

HAL•LEONARD®
CORPORATION
7777 W. BLUEMOUND RD. P.O.BOX 13819 MILWAUKEE, WI 53213

Visit Hal Leonard Online at
www.halleonard.com

Ànema e core
(With All My Heart)

Registration 3
Rhythm: Rhumba or Latin

English Lyric by Mann Curtis and Harry Akst
Italian Lyric by Tito Manlio
Music by Salve d'Esposito

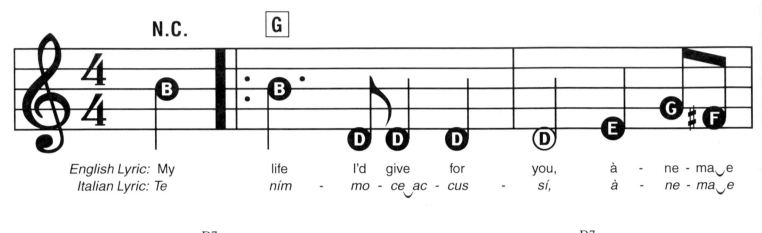

English Lyric: My life I'd give for you, à - ne - ma e
Italian Lyric: Te ním - mo ce ac cus - sí, à - ne - ma e

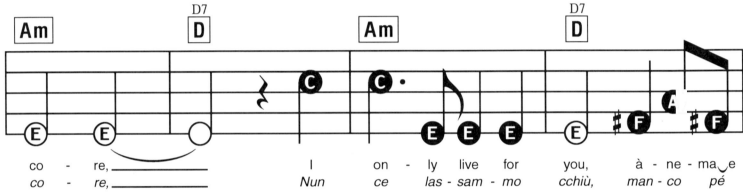

co - re, _____ I on - ly live for you, à - ne - ma e
co - re, _____ Nun ce las - sam - mo cchiù, man - co pé

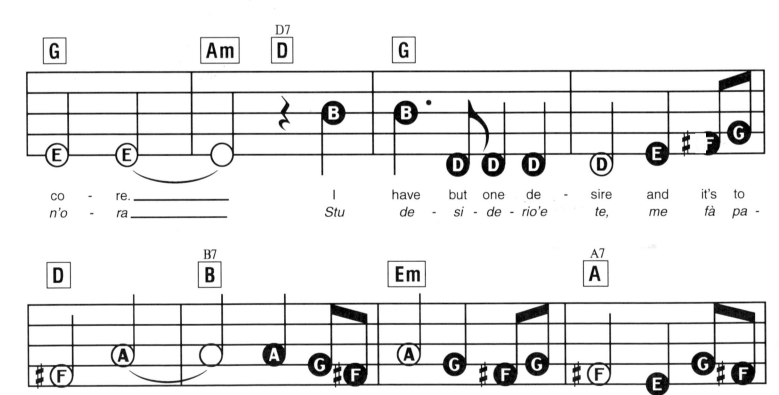

co - re. _____ I have but one de - sire and it's to
n'o - ra _____ Stu de - si - de - rio'e te, me fà pa -

love you _____ with all my heart, with all my soul, my whole life
u - ra, _____ Cam - pá cu te! Sem - pe cu te! pè nun mu -

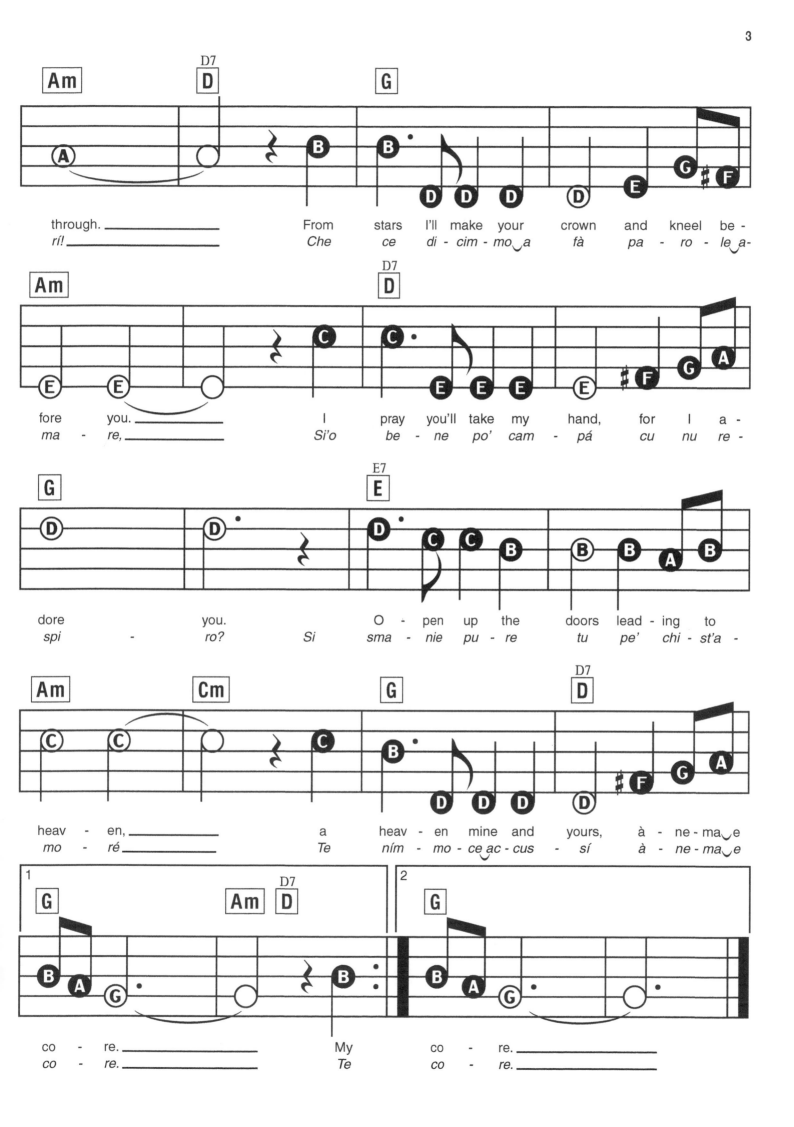

3

Arrivederci, Roma
(Goodbye to Rome)
from the Motion Picture SEVEN HILLS OF ROME

Registration 3
Rhythm: Latin

Written by Carl Sigman, Ranucci Renato,
Sandro Giovanni and Peidro Garinei

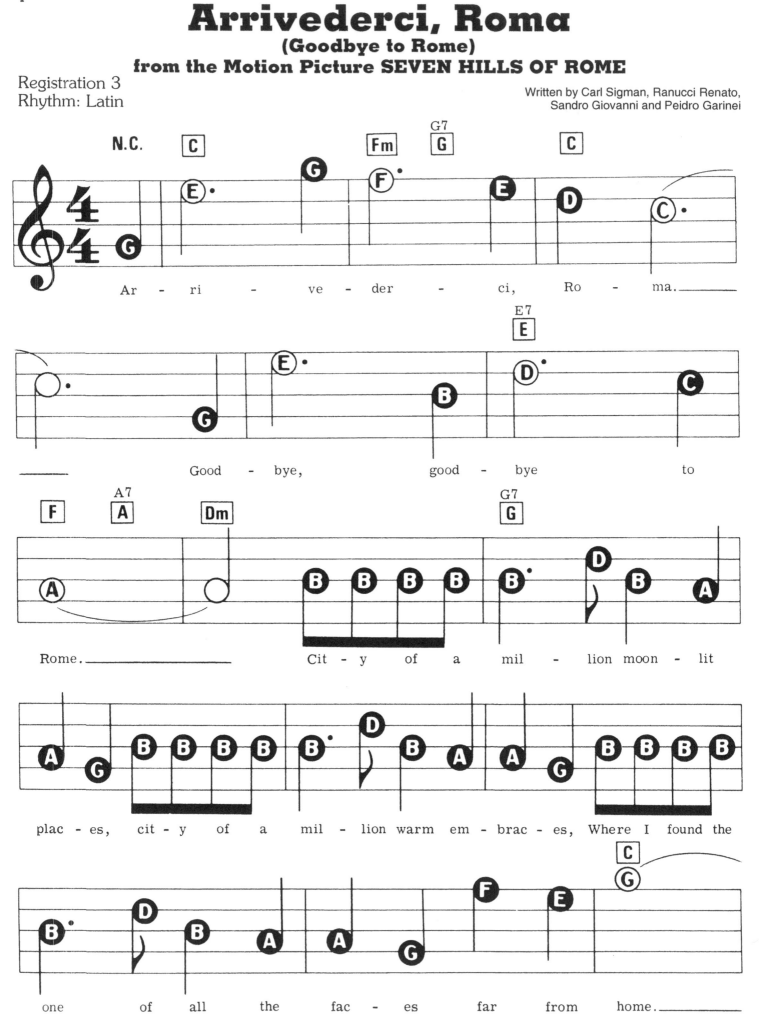

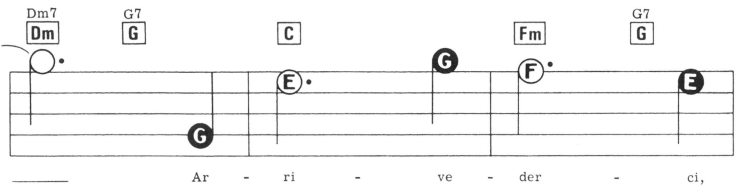

Ar - ri - ve - der - ci,

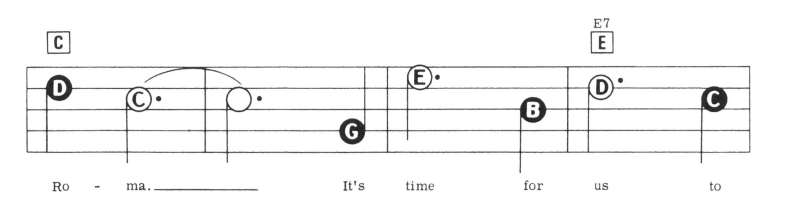

Ro - ma._____ It's time for us to

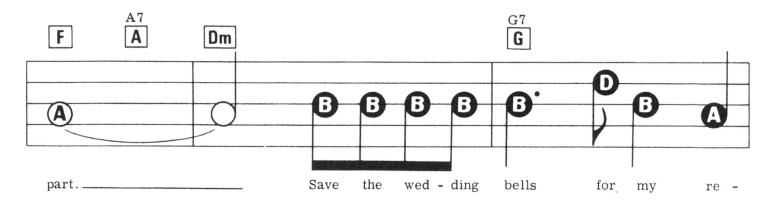

part._____ Save the wed - ding bells for my re -

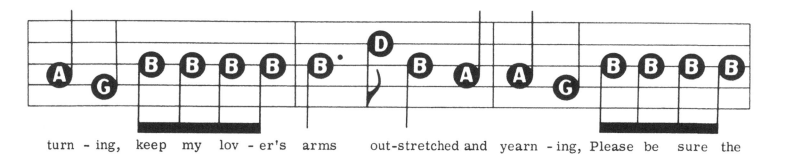

turn - ing, keep my lov - er's arms out-stretched and yearn - ing, Please be sure the

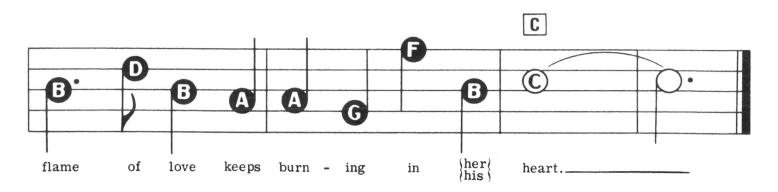

flame of love keeps burn - ing in {her}{his} heart._____

Bella notte
(This Is the Night)
from Walt Disney's LADY AND THE TRAMP

Registration 7
Rhythm: Fox Trot or Swing

Words and Music by Peggy Lee
and Sonny Burke

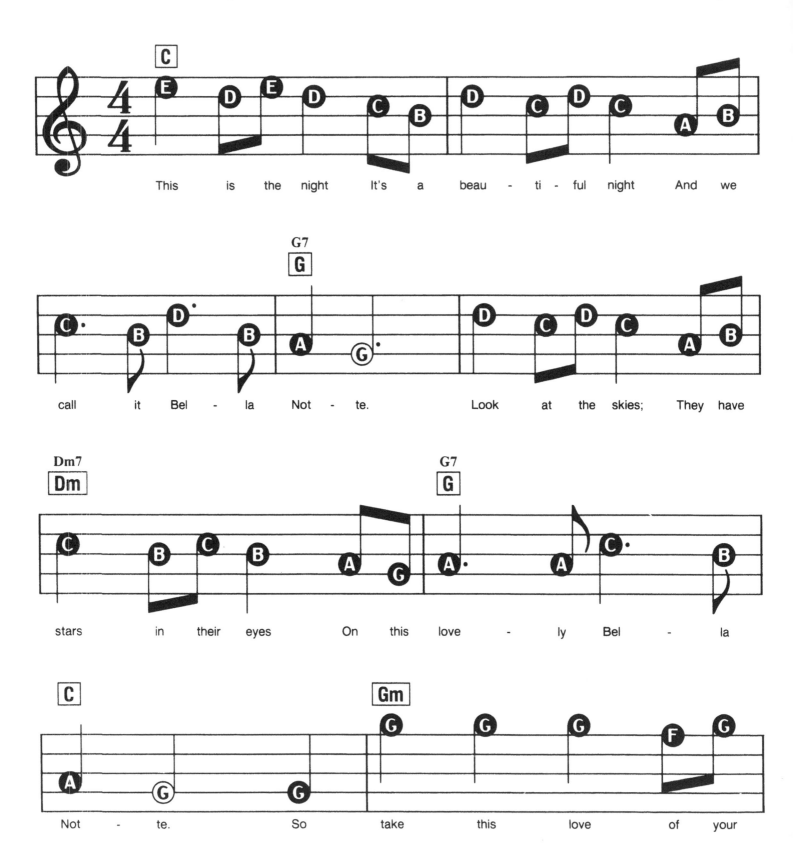

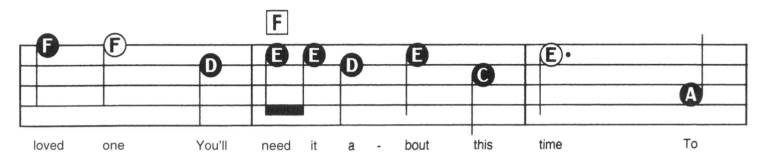

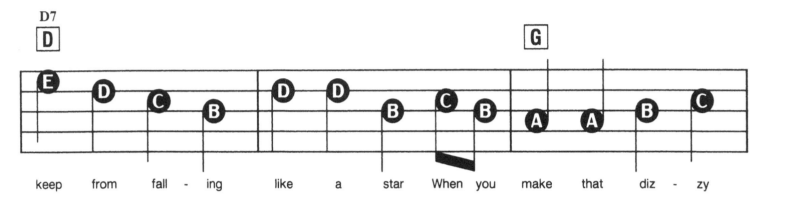

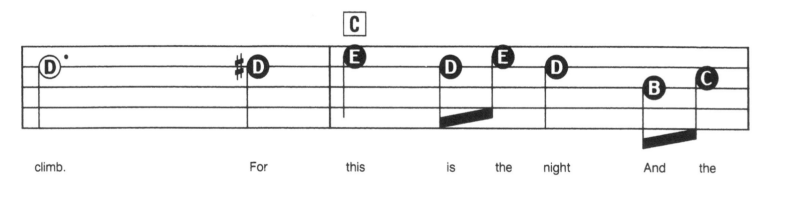

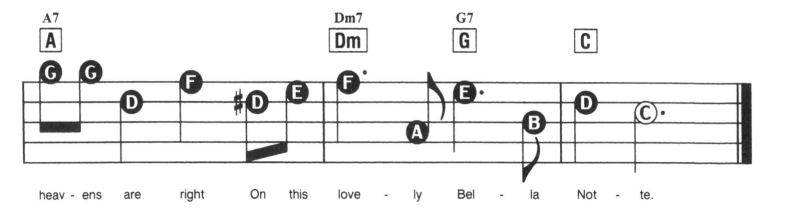

Cara, mia

Registration 3
Rhythm: Waltz

By Julio Trapani
and Lee Lange

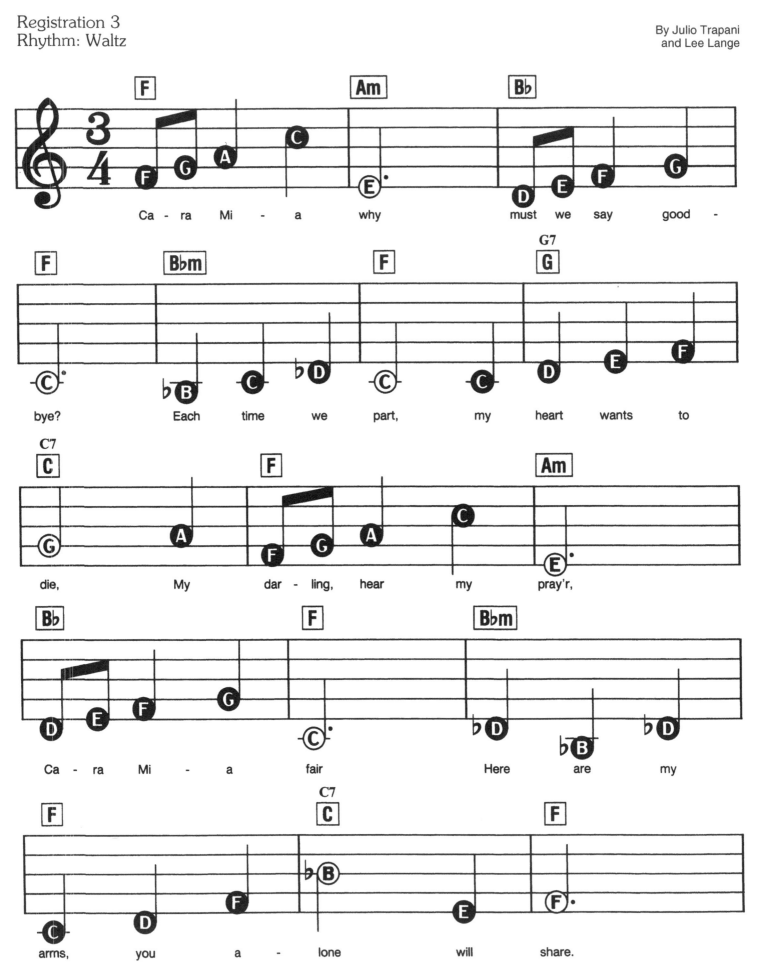

Cinema Paradiso

from CINEMA PARADISO

Registration 1
Rhythm: 4/4 Ballad or 8 Beat

Music by Ennio Morricone

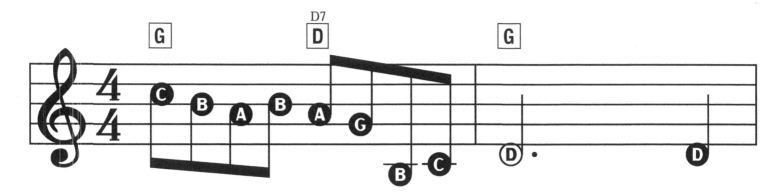

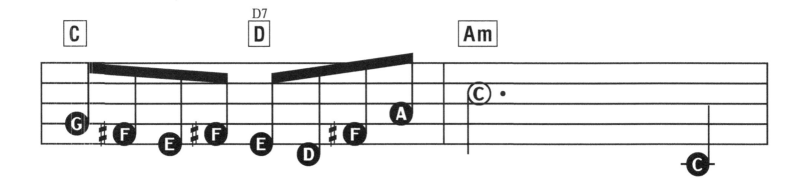

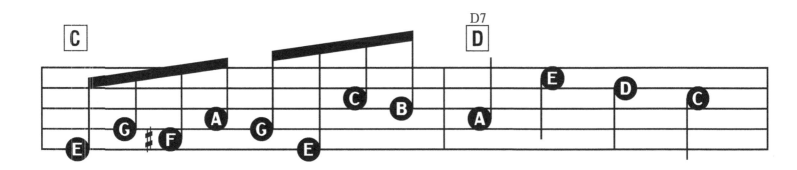

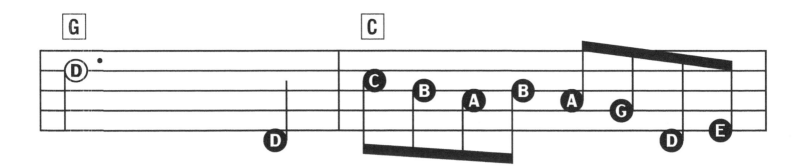

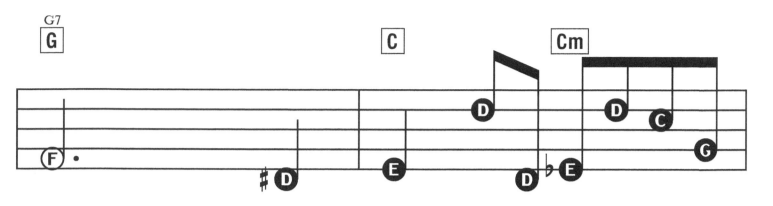

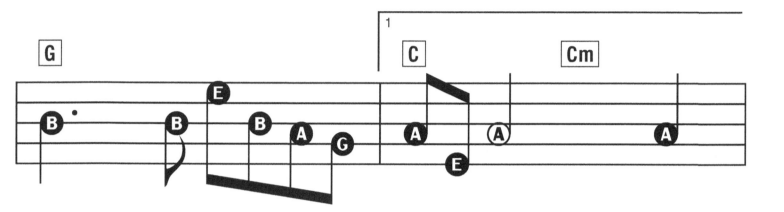

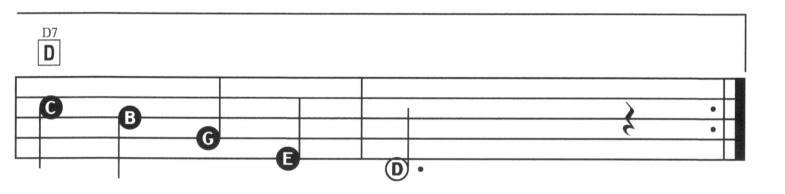

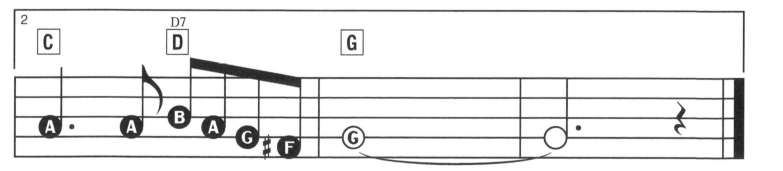

Isle of Capri

Registration 8
Rhythm: Bossa Nova or Latin

Words by Jimmy Kennedy
Music by Will Grosz

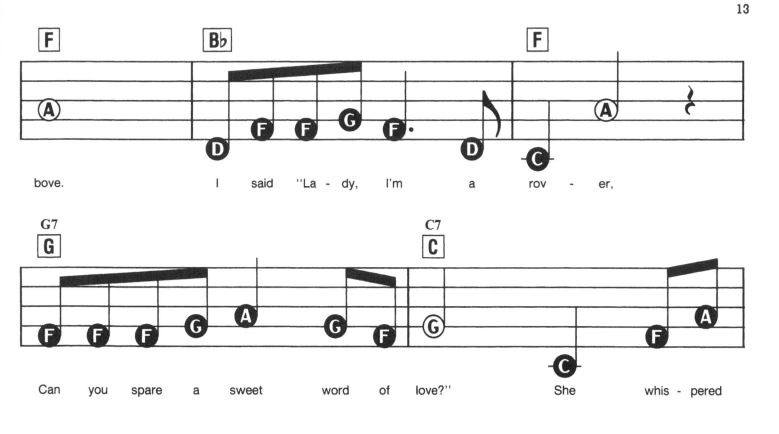

bove.   I said "La - dy, I'm   a   rov - er,

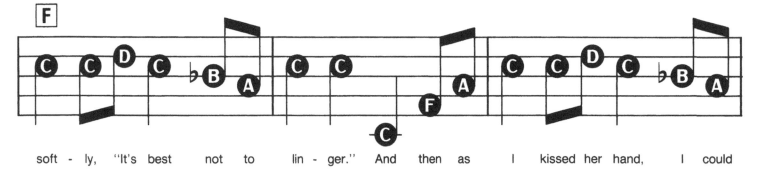

Can   you   spare   a   sweet   word   of   love?"   She   whis - pered

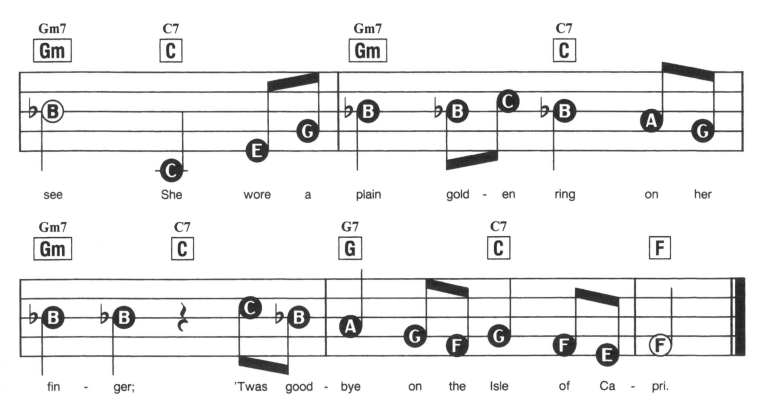

soft - ly,   "It's   best   not   to   lin - ger."   And   then   as   I   kissed   her   hand,   I   could

see   She   wore   a   plain   gold - en   ring   on   her

fin - ger;   'Twas   good - bye   on   the   Isle   of   Ca - pri.

Mambo Italiano

Registration 7
Rhythm: Mambo or Latin

Words and Music by
Bob Merrill

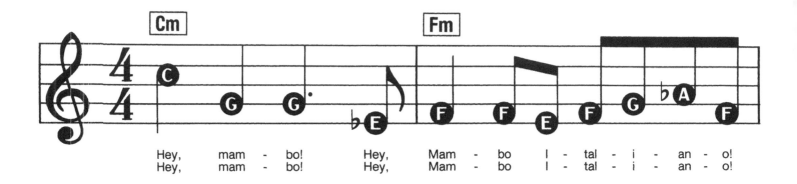

Hey, mam - bo! Hey, Mam - bo I - tal - i - an - o!
Hey, mam - bo! Hey, Mam - bo I - tal - i - an - o!

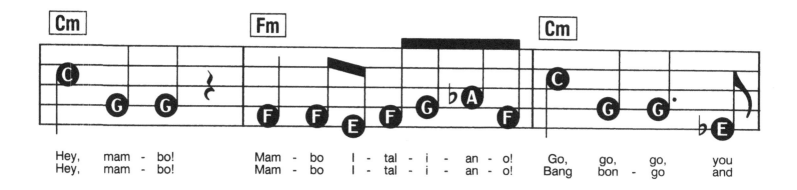

Hey, mam - bo! Mam - bo I - tal - i - an - o! Go, go, go, you
Hey, mam - bo! Mam - bo I - tal - i - an - o! Bang bon - go and

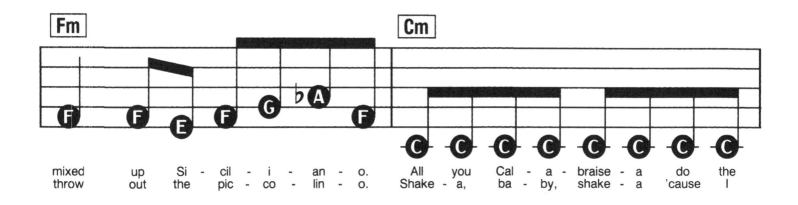

mixed up Si - cil - i - an - o. All you Cal - a - braise - a do the
throw out the pic - co - lin - o. Shake - a, ba - by, shake - a 'cause I

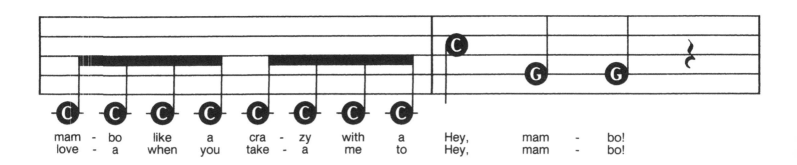

mam - bo like a cra - zy with a Hey, mam - bo!
love - a when you take - a me to Hey, mam - bo!

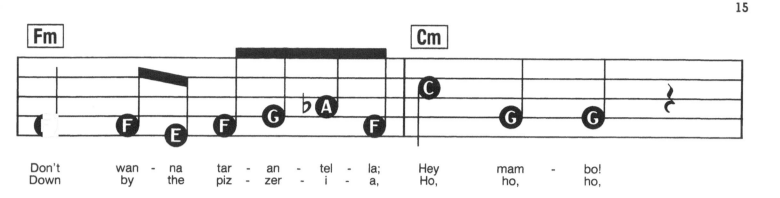

Don't wan - na tar - an - tel - la; Hey mam - bo!
Down by the piz - zer - i - a, Ho, ho, ho,

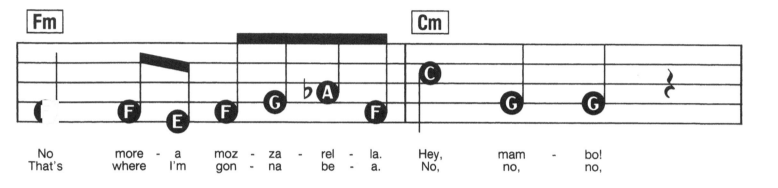

No more - a moz - za - rel - la. Hey, mam - bo!
That's where I'm gon - na be - a. No, no, no,

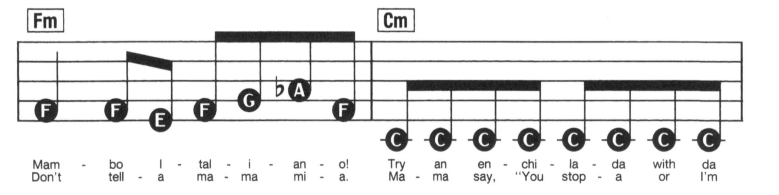

Mam - bo I - tal - i - an - o! Try an en - chi - la - da with da
Don't tell - a ma - ma mi - a. Ma - ma say, "You stop - a or I'm

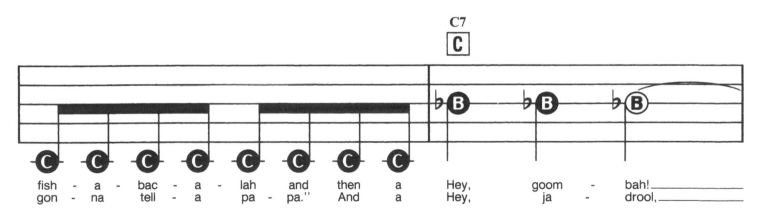

fish - a - bac - a - lah and then a Hey, goom - bah!_____
gon - na tell - a pa - pa." And a Hey, ja - drool,_____

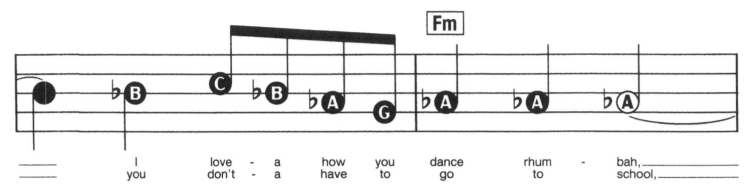

I love - a how you dance rhum - bah,_____
you don't - a how have to go to school,_____

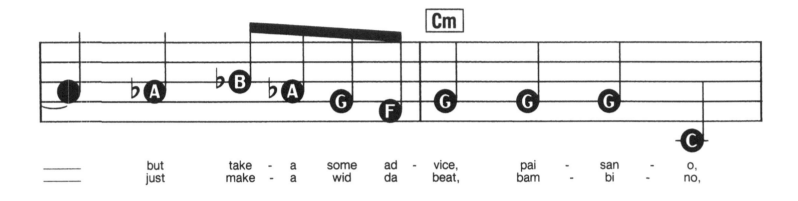

_____ but take - a some ad - vice, pai - san - o,
_____ just make - a wid da beat, bam - bi - no,

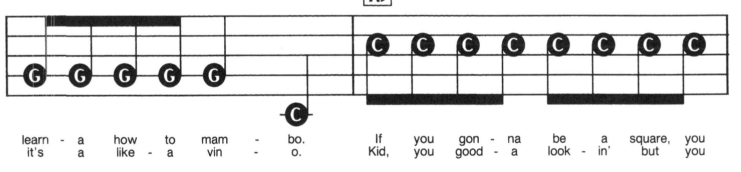

learn - a how to mam - bo. If you gon - na be a square, you
it's a like - a vin - o. Kid, you good - a look - in' but you

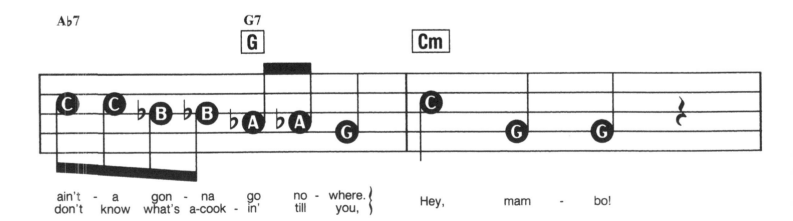

ain't - a gon - na go no - where. } Hey, mam - bo!
don't know what's a-cook - in' till you, }

A Man Without Love
(Quando m'innamoro)

Registration 8
Rhythm: Fox Trot or Swing

English Lyric by Barry Mason
Original Words and Music by D. Pace, M. Panzeri and R. Livraghi

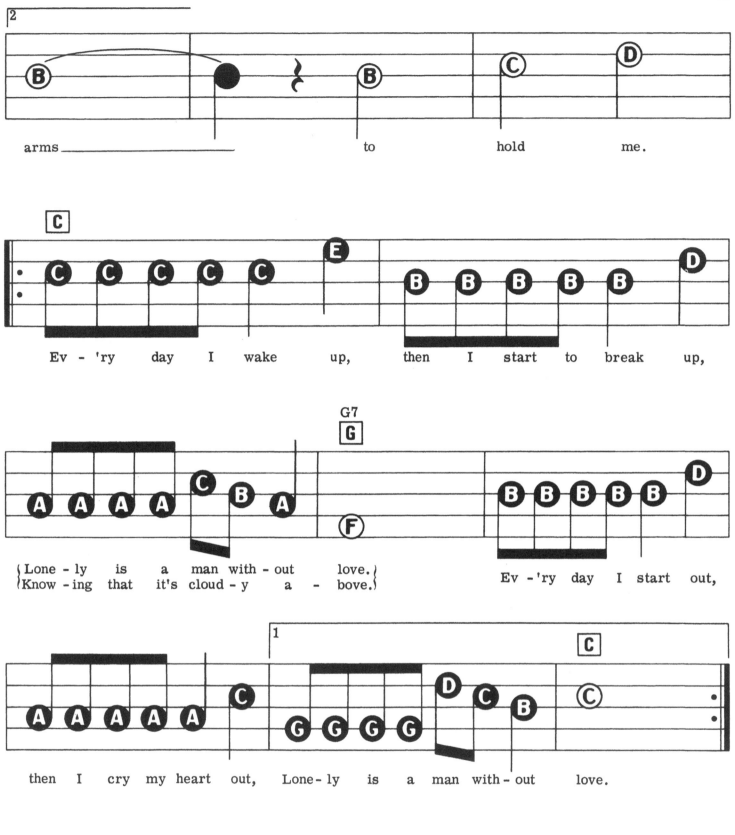

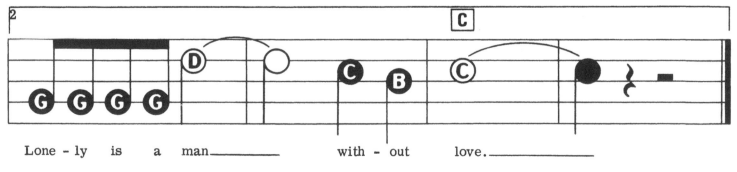

Mona Lisa
from the Paramount Picture CAPTAIN CAREY, U.S.A.

Registration 9
Rhythm: Swing or 8 Beat

Words and Music by Jay Livingston
and Ray Evans

More
(Ti guarderò nel cuore)
from the Film MONDO CANE

Music by Nino Oliviero and Riz Ortolani
Italian Lyrics by Marcello Ciorciolini
English Lyrics by Norman Newell

Registration 2
Rhythm: Bossa Nova or Latin

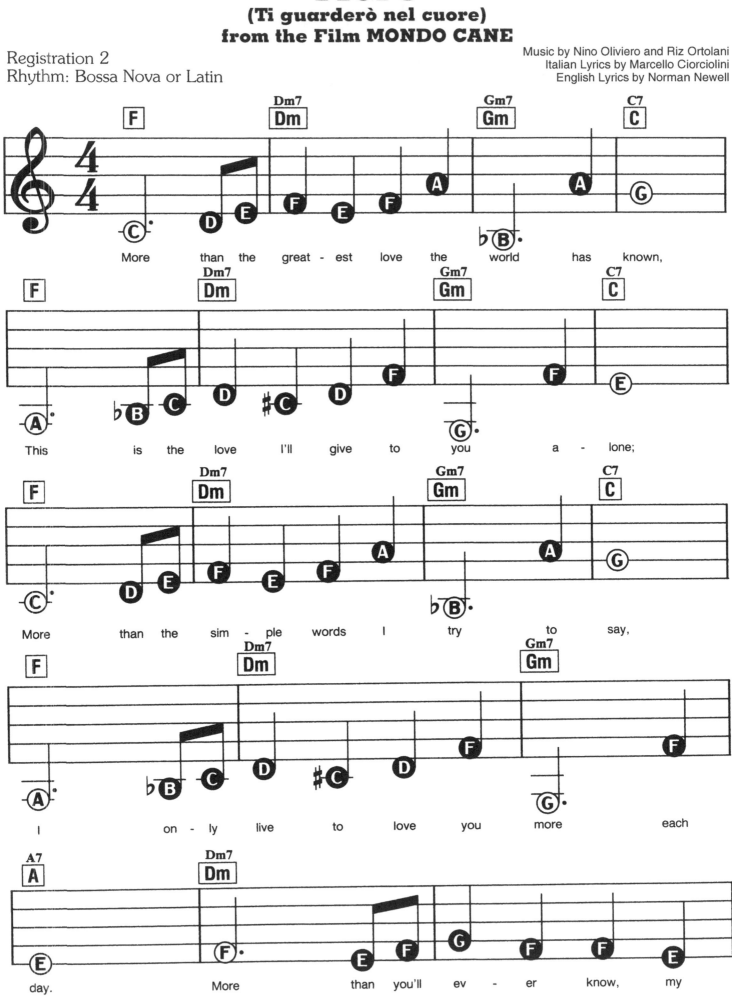

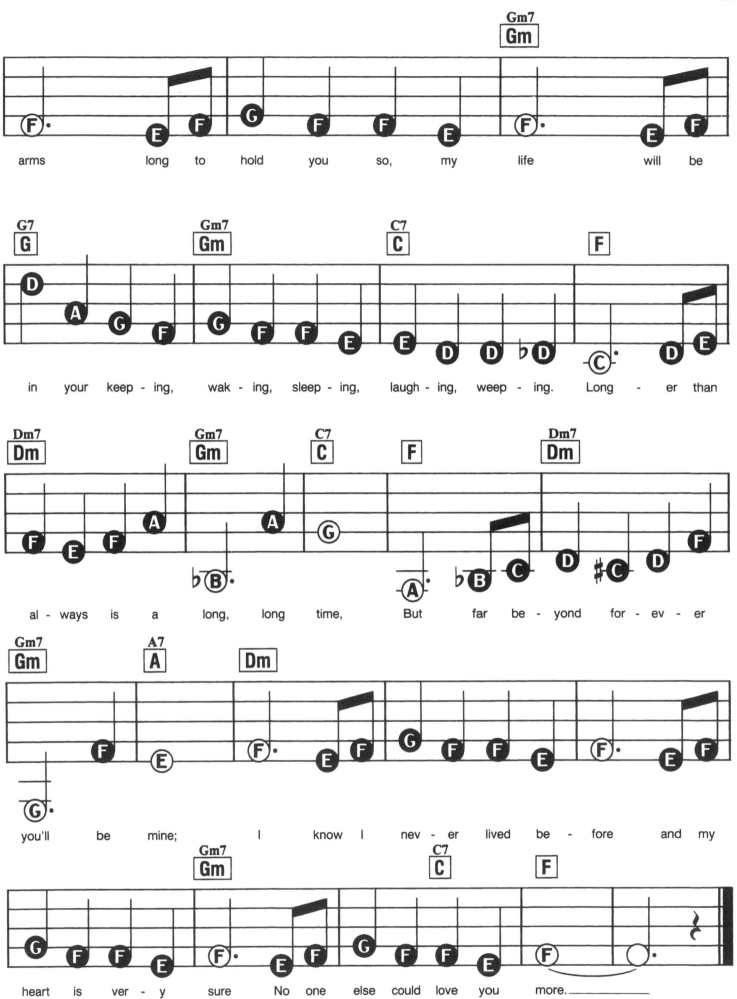

My Way

Registration 5
Rhythm: Ballad or Rock

English Words by Paul Anka
Original French Words by Gilles Thibault
Music by Jacques Revaux and Claude Francois

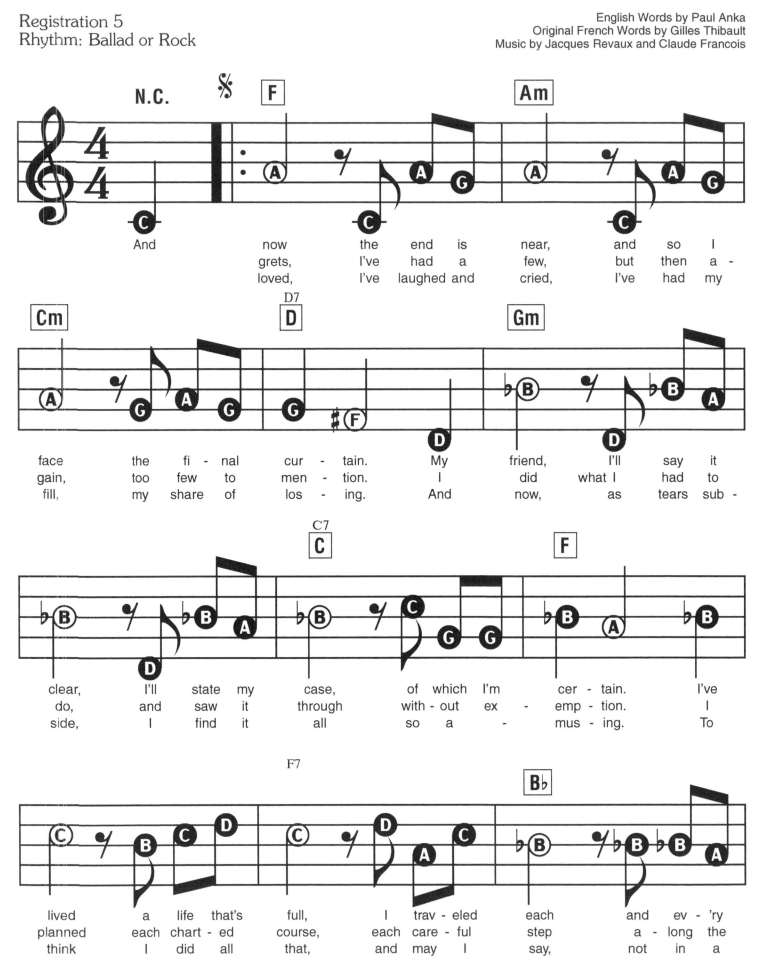

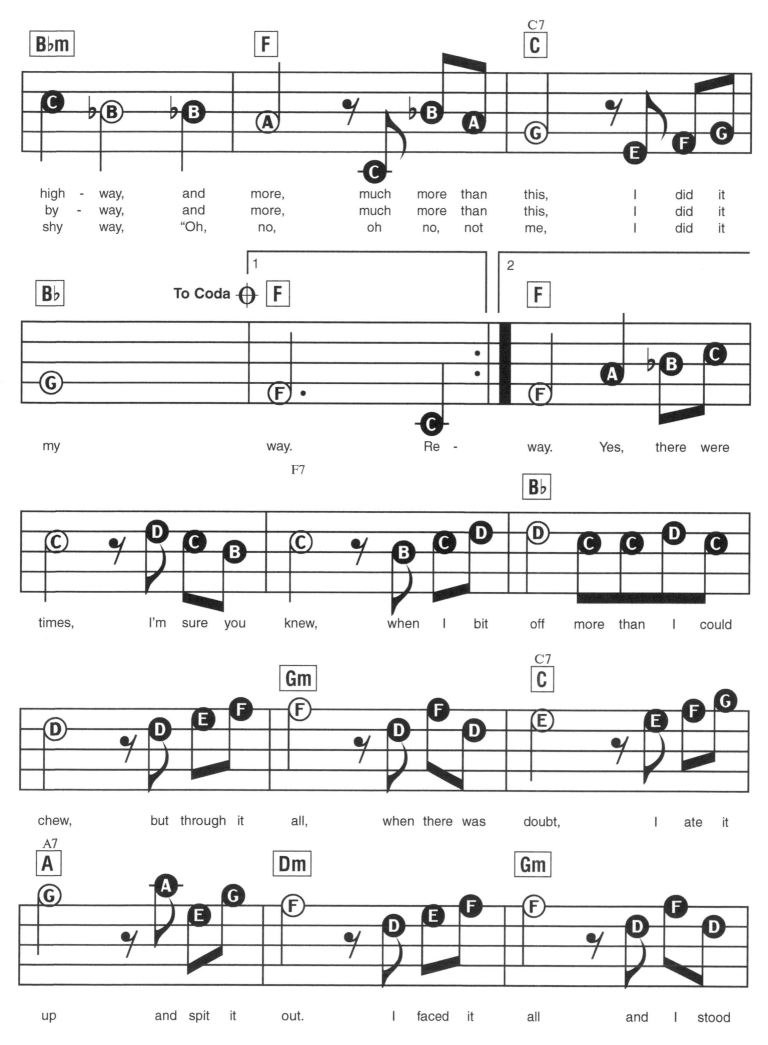

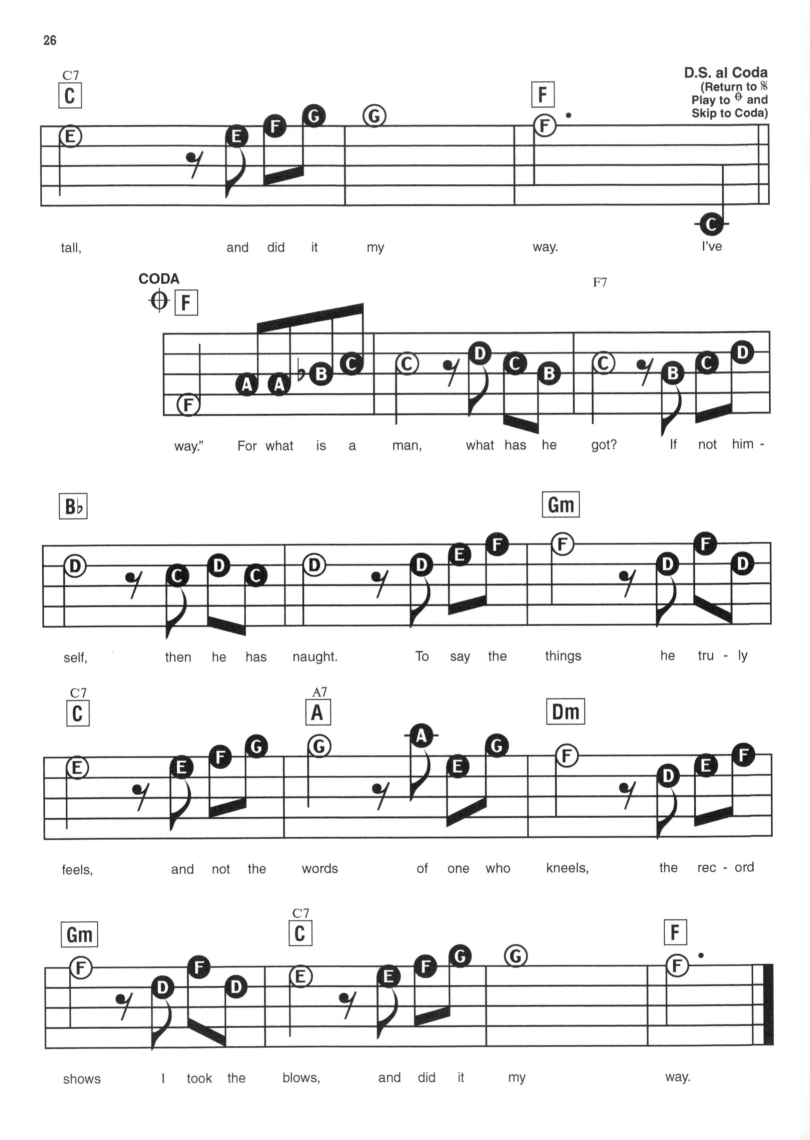

D.S. al Coda
(Return to %
Play to ⊕ and
Skip to Coda)

tall,   and   did   it   my   way.   I've

CODA

way."   For   what   is   a   man,   what   has   he   got?   If   not   him -

self,   then   he   has   naught.   To   say   the   things   he   tru - ly

feels,   and   not   the   words   of   one   who   kneels,   the   rec - ord

shows   I   took   the   blows,   and   did   it   my   way.

Never on Sunday
from Jules Dassin's Motion Picture NEVER ON SUNDAY

Registration 1
Rhythm: Latin

Words by Billy Towne
Music by Manos Hadjidakis

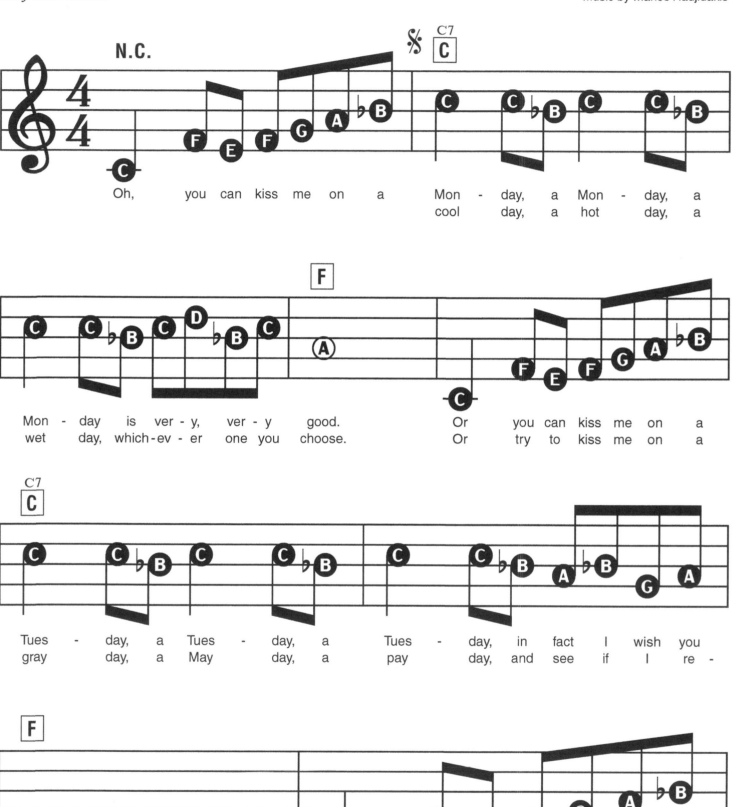

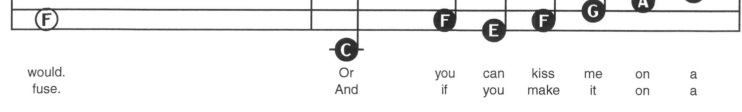

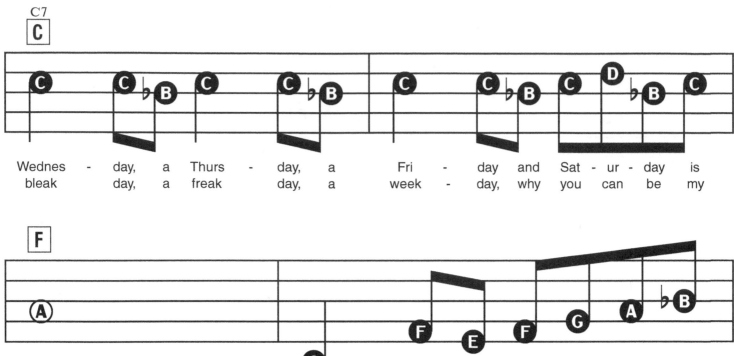

Wednes - day, a Thurs - day, a Fri - day and Sat - ur - day is
bleak day, a freak day, a week - day, why you can be my

best, But nev - er, nev - er on a
guest. But nev - er, nev - er on a

To Coda

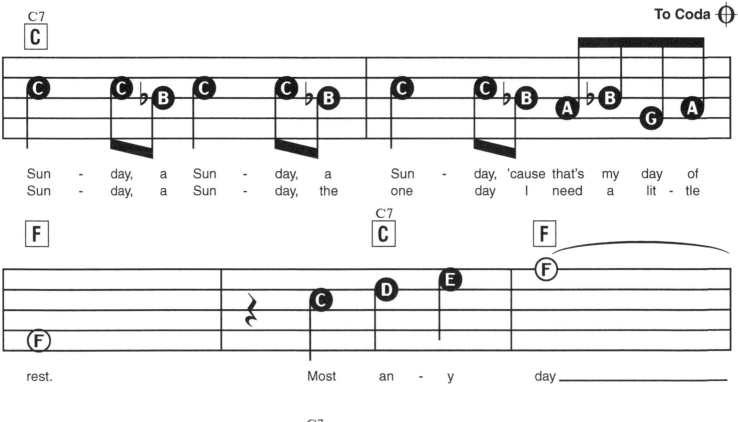

Sun - day, a Sun - day, a Sun - day, 'cause that's my day of
Sun - day, a Sun - day, the one day I need a lit - tle

rest. Most an - y day _____

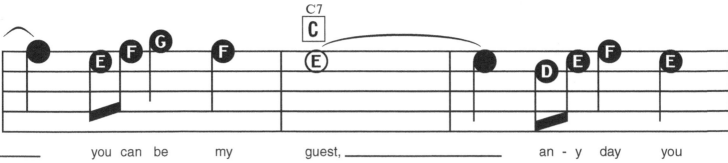

_____ you can be my guest, _____ an - y day you

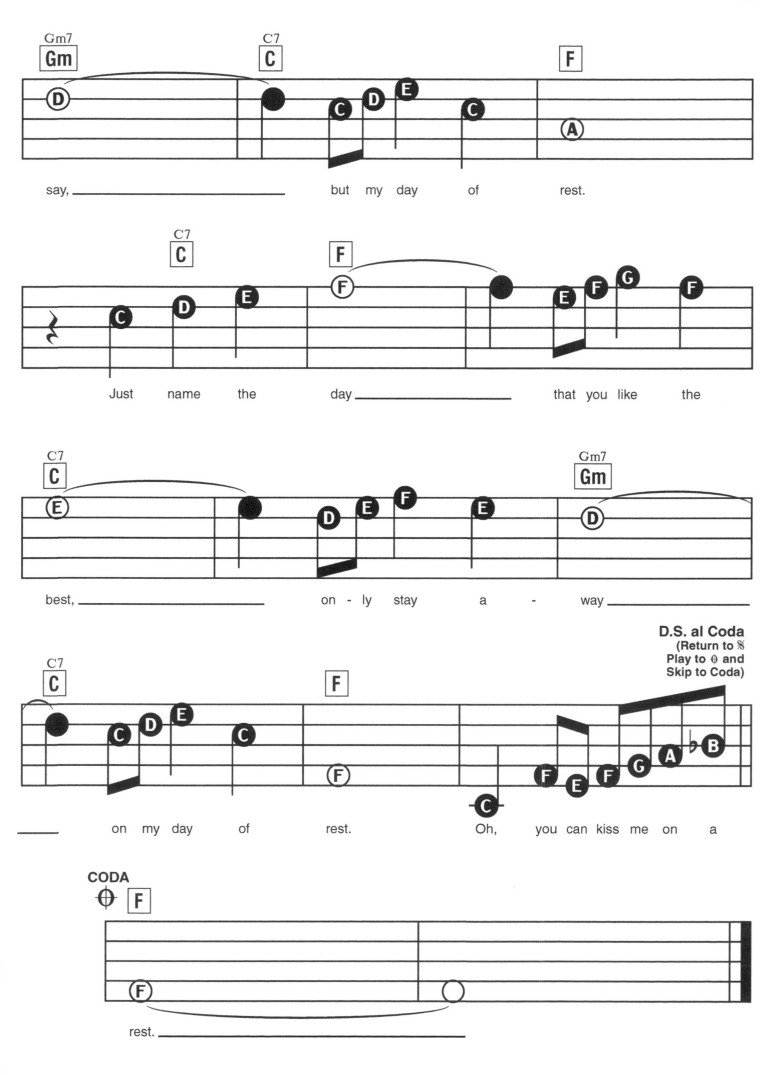

Non dimenticar
(T'ho voluto bene)
from the Film ANNA

English Lyric by Shelley Dobbins
Original Italian Lyrics by Michele Galdieri
Music by P.G. Redi

Registration 2
Rhythm: Latin

Non di-men-ti-car means don't for-get you are my dar-ling,____
Non di-men-ti-car my love is like a star, my dar-ling,____

____ Don't for-get to be _____ all you mean to
____ Shin-ing bright and clear _____

me. _____ ____ Just be-cause you're

here. _____ Please do not for-get that our lips have

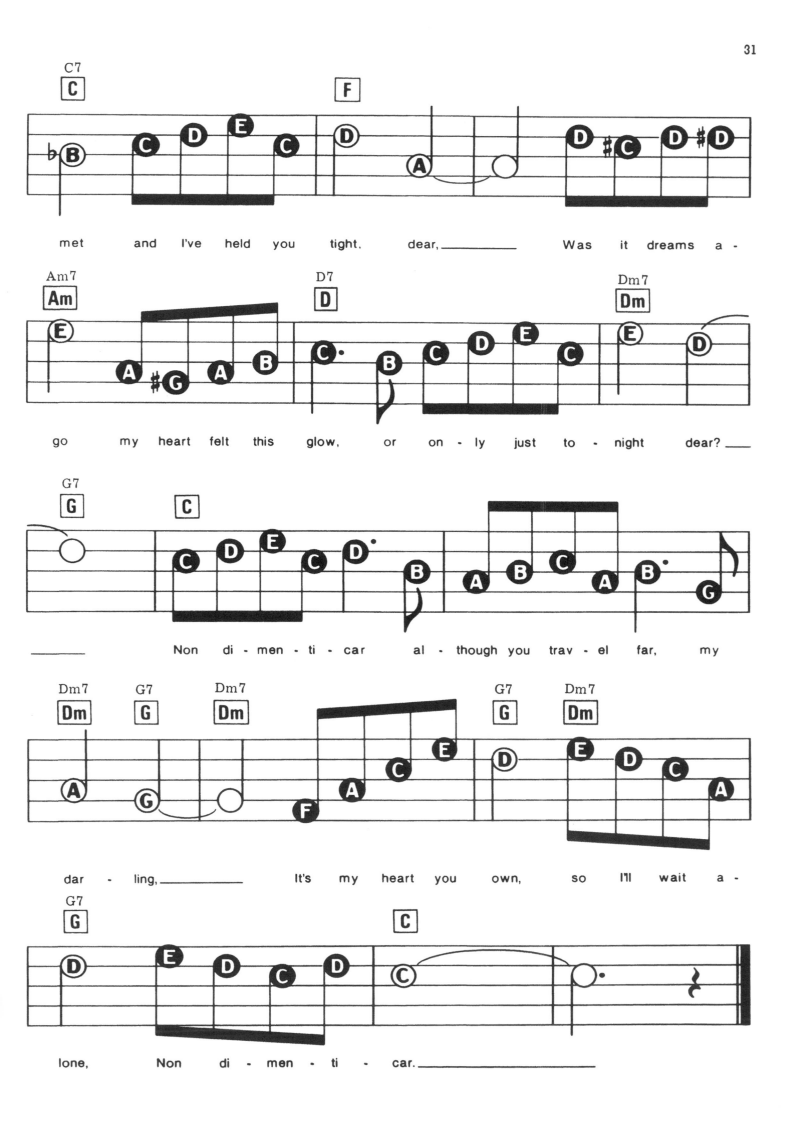

met   and   I've   held   you   tight,   dear,_____   Was   it   dreams   a -

go   my   heart   felt   this   glow,   or   on - ly   just   to - night   dear?____

_____   Non   di - men - ti - car   al - though   you   trav - el   far,   my

dar - ling,_____   It's   my   heart   you   own,   so   I'll   wait   a -

lone,   Non   di - men - ti - car._____

Que sera, sera
(Whatever Will Be, Will Be)
from THE MAN WHO KNEW TOO MUCH

Registration 10
Rhythm: Waltz

Words and Music by Jay Livingston
and Ray Evans

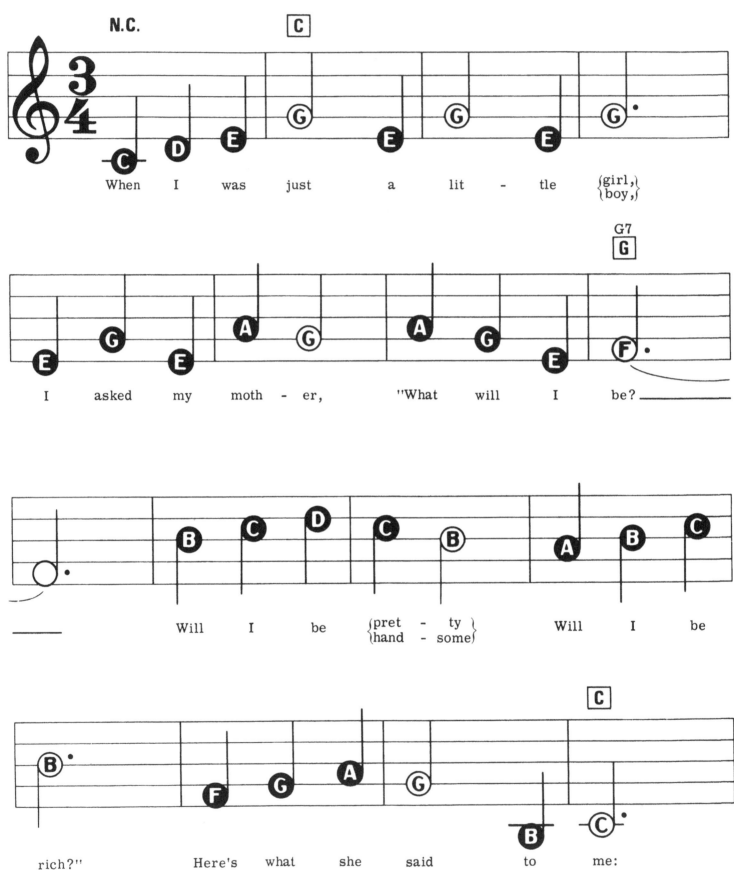

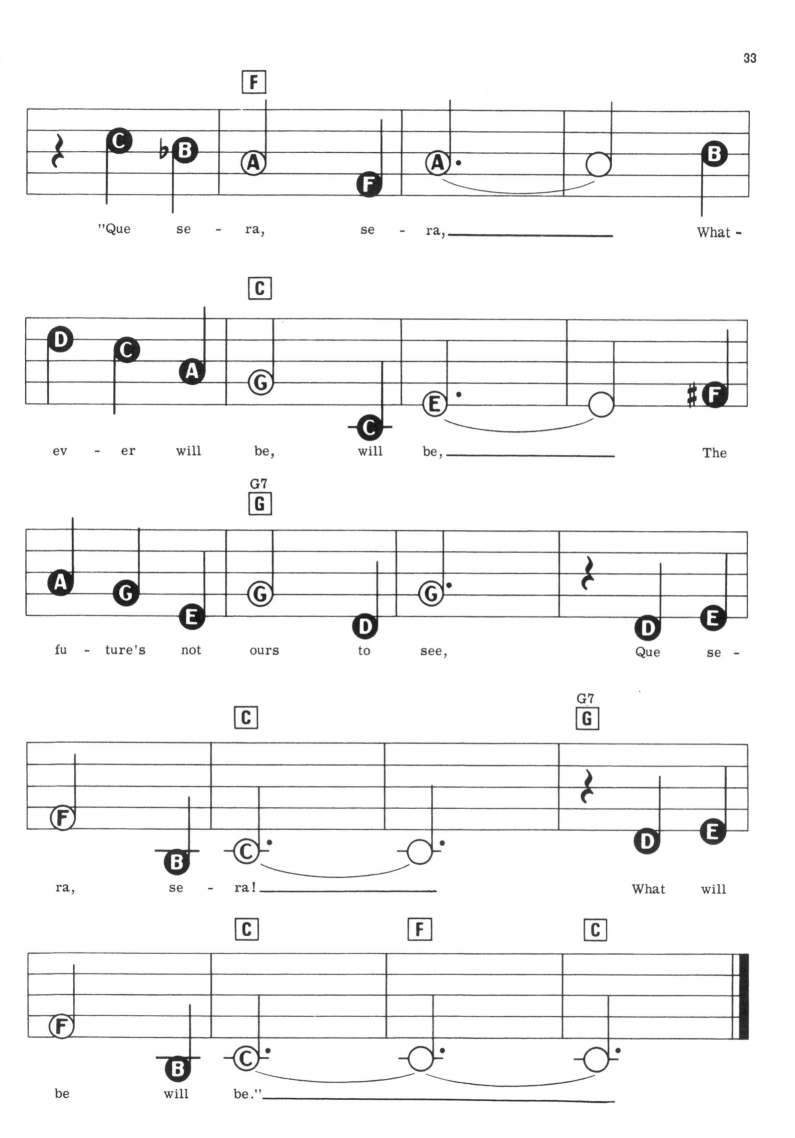

33

Speak Softly, Love
(Love Theme)
from the Paramount Picture THE GODFATHER

Registration 1
Rhythm: Ballad or Slow Rock

Words by Larry Kusik
Music by Nino Rota

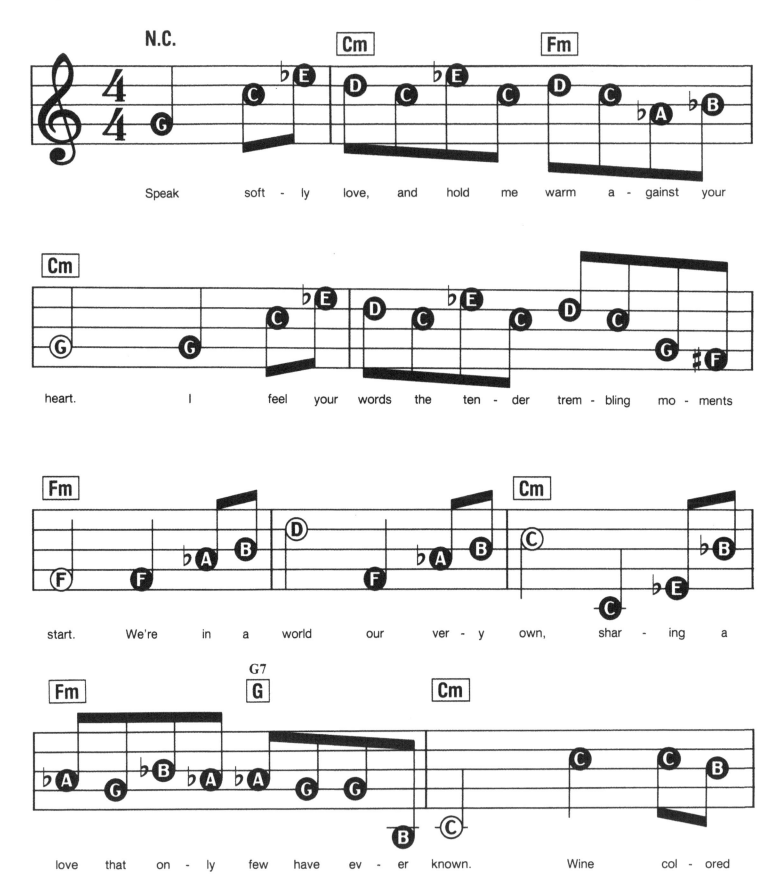

days warmed by the sun, deep vel - vet nights when we are

one. Speak soft - ly love, so no one hears us but the

sky. The vows of love we make will live un - til we

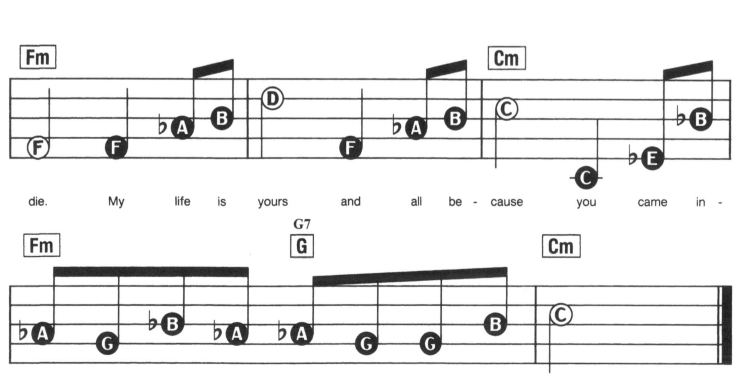

die. My life is yours and all be - cause you came in -

to my world with love so soft - ly love.

Strangers in the Night
adapted from A MAN COULD GET KILLED

Registration 5
Rhythm: Ballad or Slow Rock

Words by Charles Singleton and Eddie Snyder
Music by Bert Kaempfert

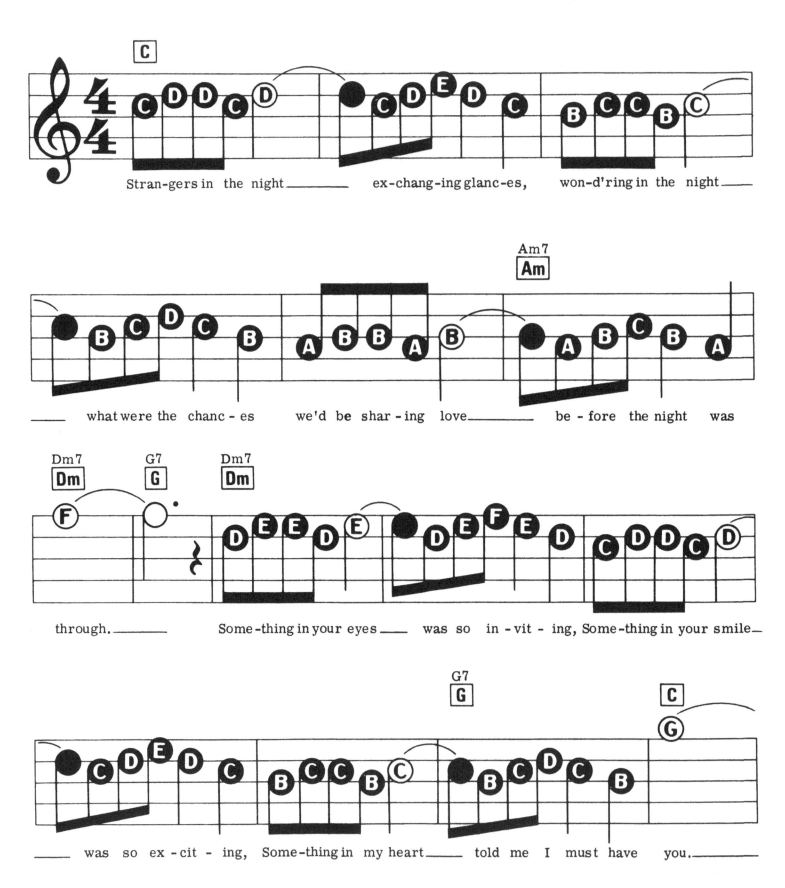

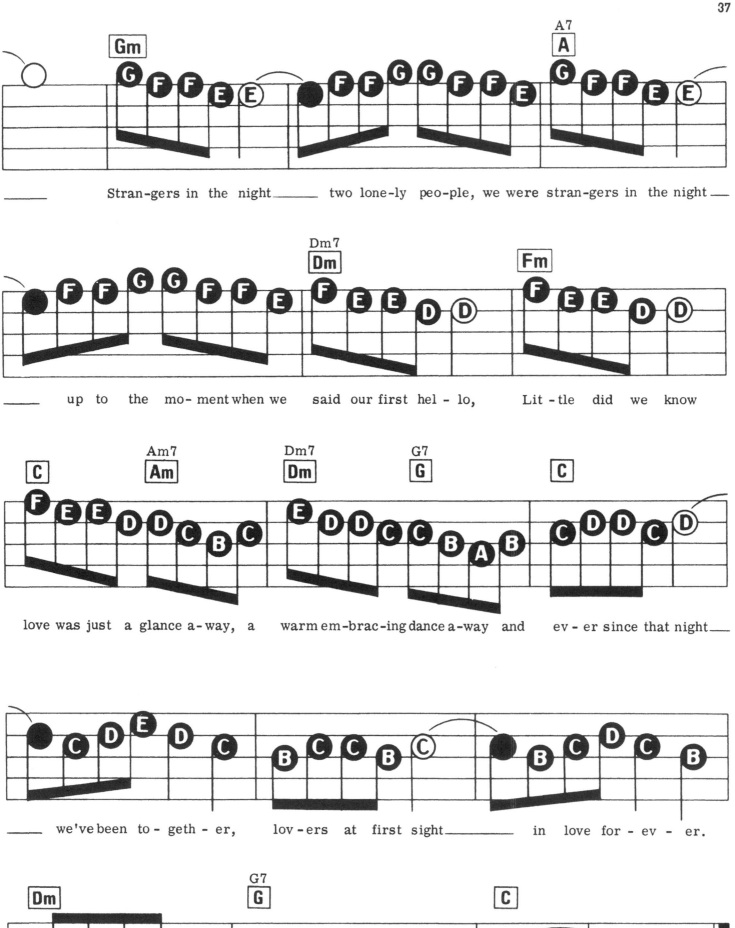

Stran-gers in the night_____ two lone-ly peo-ple, we were stran-gers in the night ___

___ up to the mo-ment when we said our first hel - lo, Lit -tle did we know

love was just a glance a-way, a warm em-brac-ing dance a-way and ev - er since that night___

___ we've been to - geth - er, lov -ers at first sight_____ in love for - ev - er.

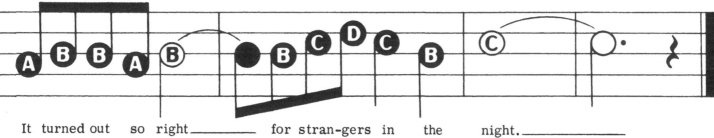

It turned out so right_____ for stran-gers in the night._____

Summertime in Venice
from the Motion Picture SUMMERTIME

Registration 9
Rhythm: Latin or Bossa Nova

English Words by Carl Sigman
Music by Icini

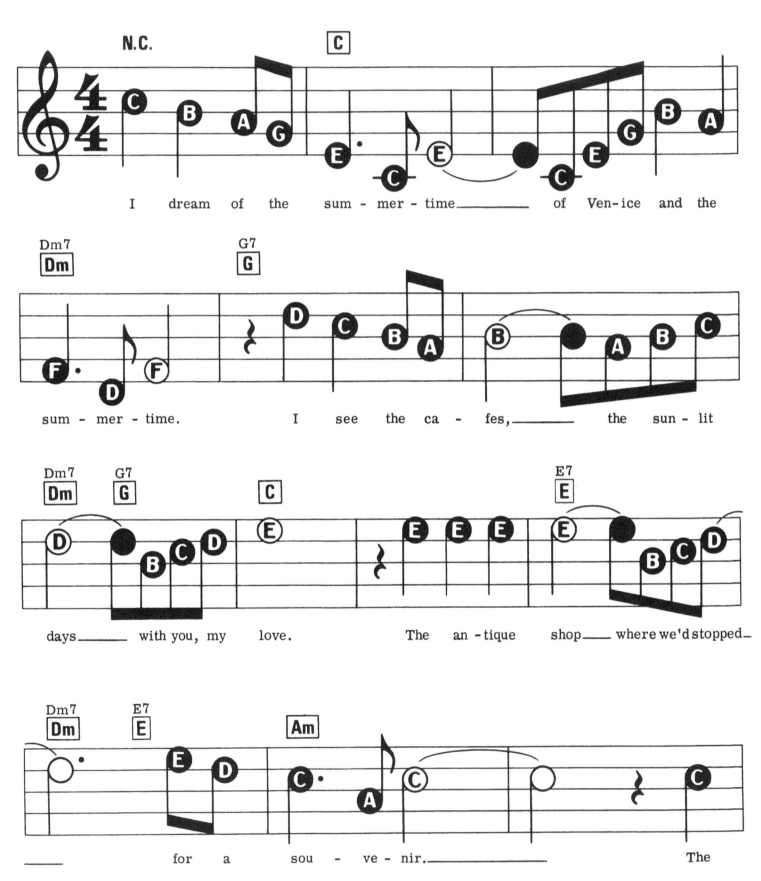

39

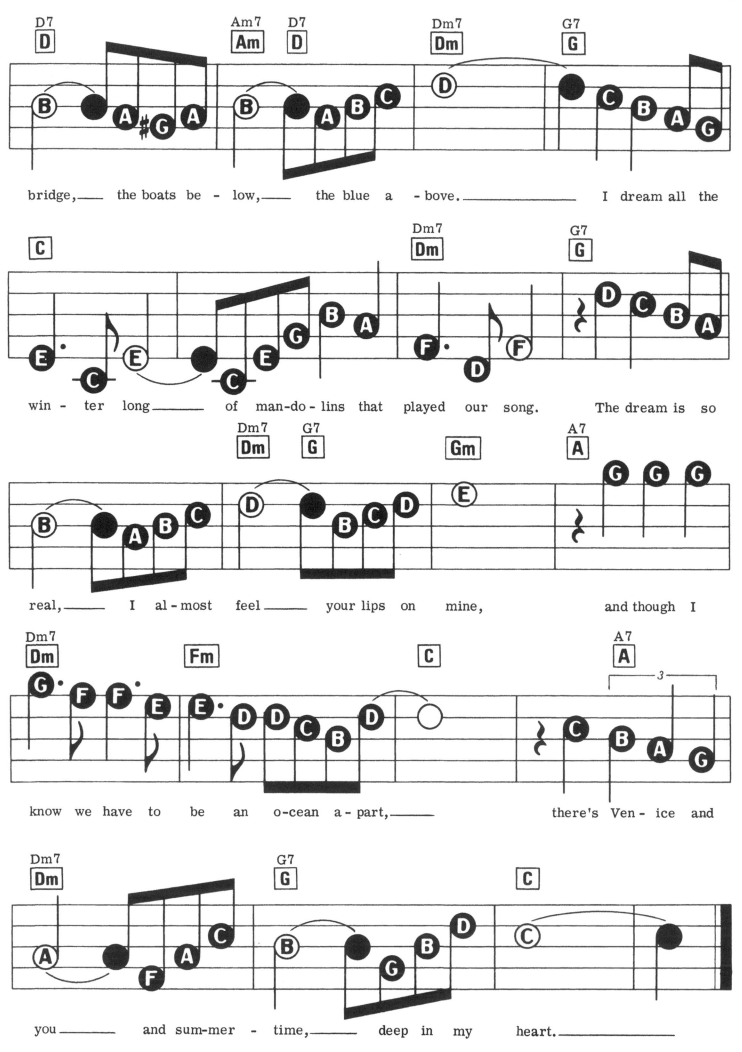

That's Amoré
(That's Love)
from the Paramount Picture THE CADDY

Registration 3
Rhythm: Waltz

Words by Jack Brooks
Music by Harry Warren

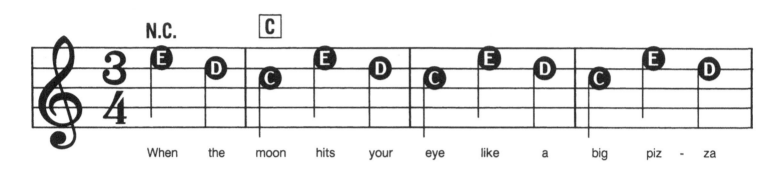

When the moon hits your eye like a big piz - za

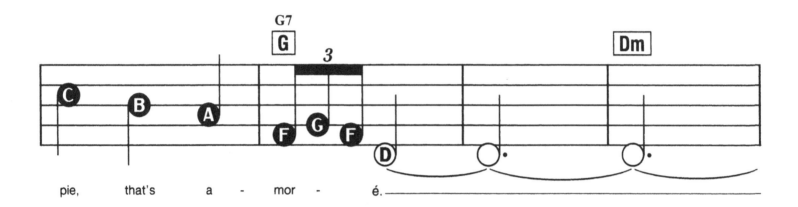

pie, that's a - mor - é. _____

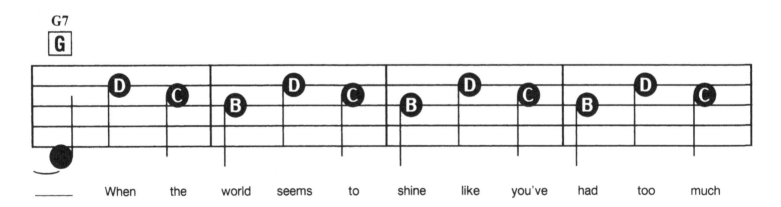

_____ When the world seems to shine like you've had too much

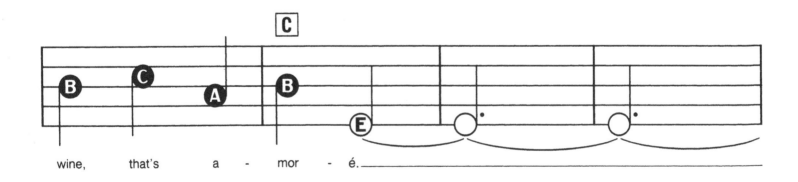

wine, that's a - mor - é. _____

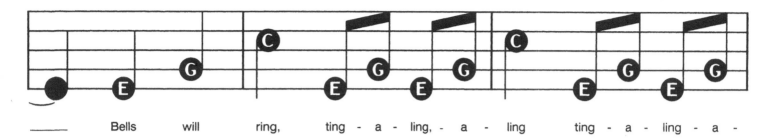

Bells will ring, ting - a - ling, - a - ling ting - a - ling - a -

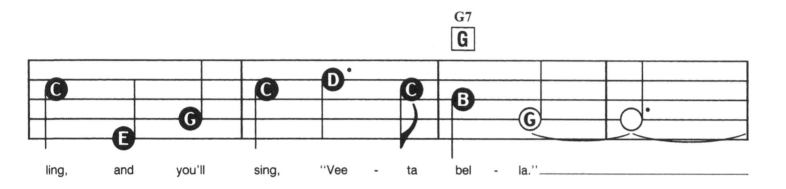

ling, and you'll sing, "Vee - ta bel - la."_____

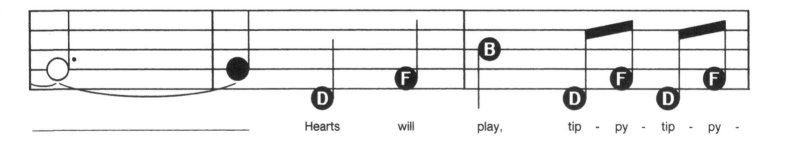

_____ Hearts will play, tip - py - tip - py -

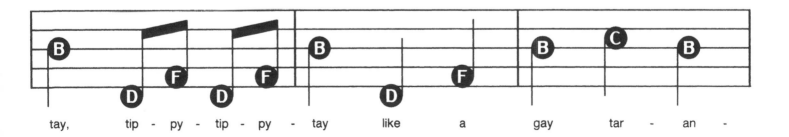

tay, tip - py - tip - py - tay like a gay tar - an -

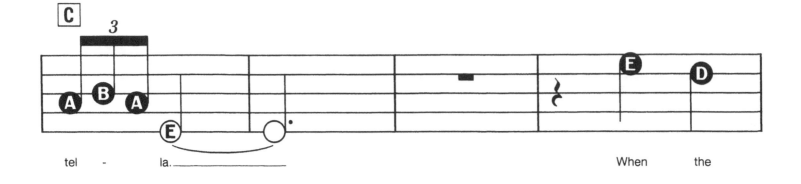

tel - la.＿＿＿＿ When the

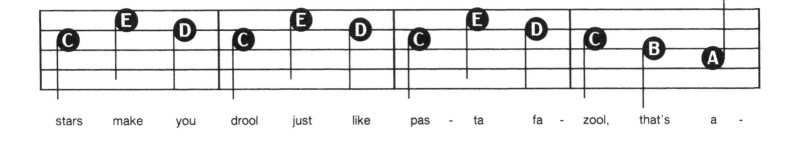

stars make you drool just like pas - ta fa - zool, that's a -

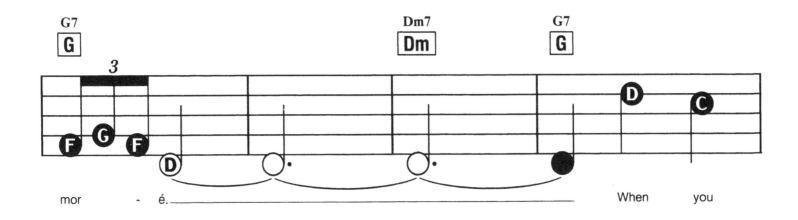

mor - é.＿＿＿＿＿＿＿＿＿ When you

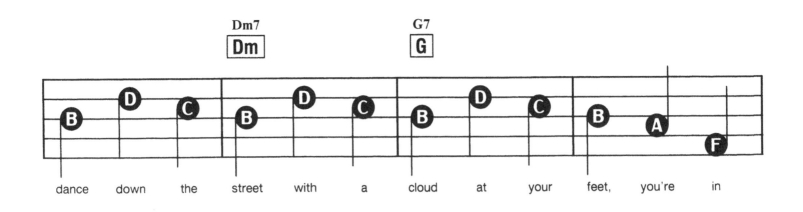

dance down the street with a cloud at your feet, you're in

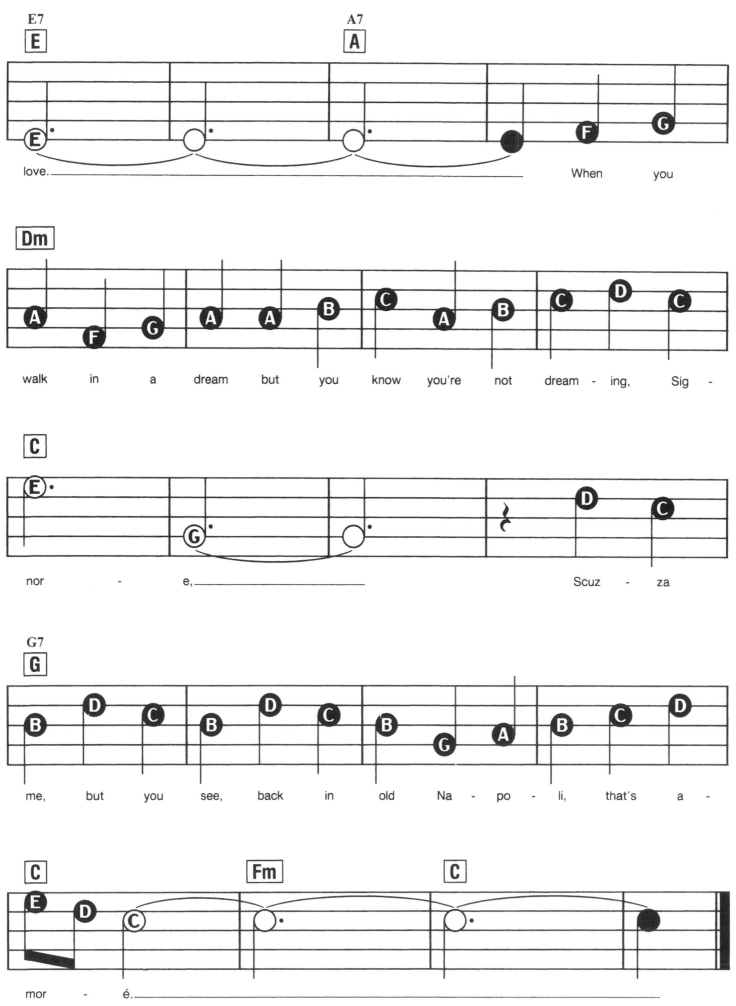

A Time for Us
(Love Theme)
from the Paramount Picture ROMEO AND JULIET

Registration 1
Rhythm: Waltz

Words by Larry Kusik and Eddie Snyder
Music by Nino Rota

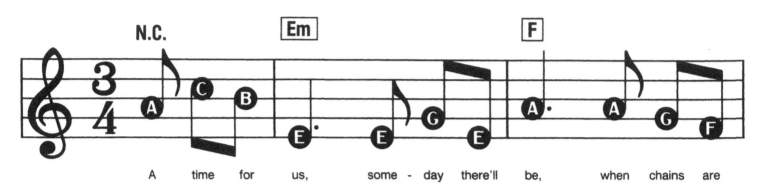

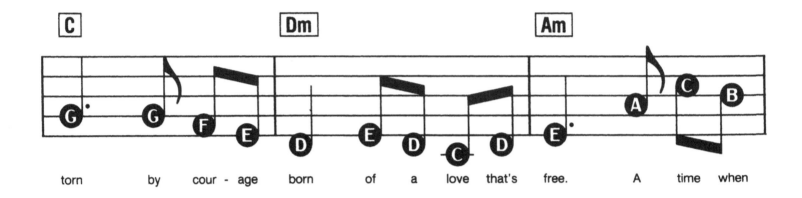

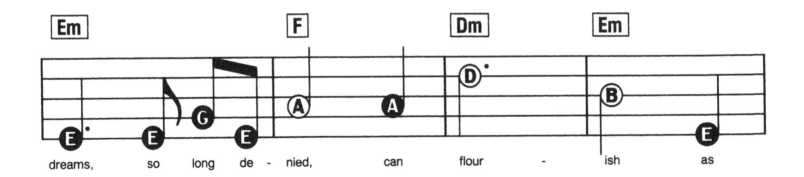

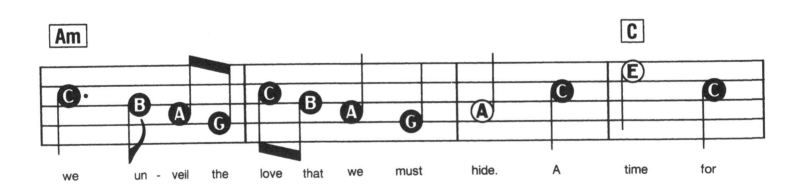

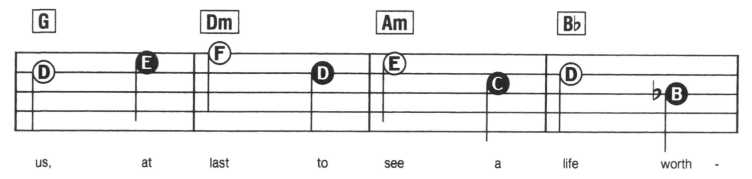

us,   at   last   to   see   a   life   worth -

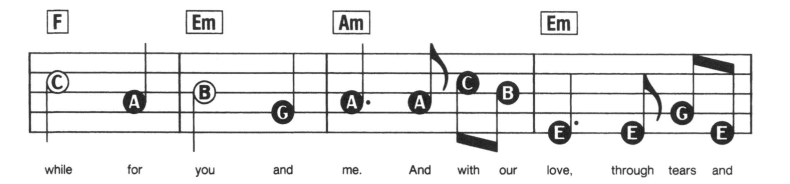

while   for   you   and   me.   And   with   our   love,   through   tears   and

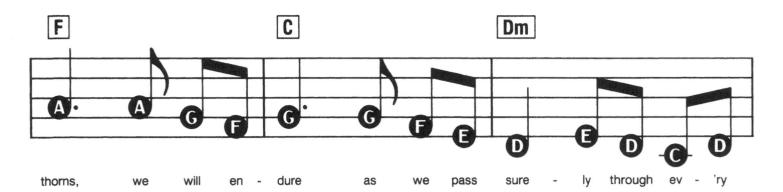

thorns,   we   will   en - dure   as   we   pass   sure - ly   through   ev - 'ry

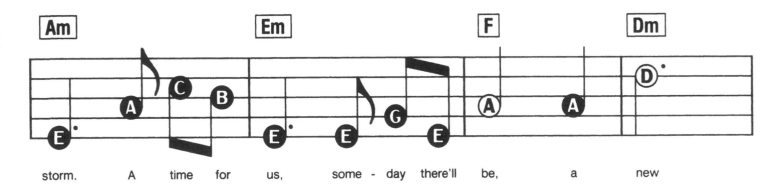

storm.   A   time   for   us,   some - day   there'll   be,   a   new

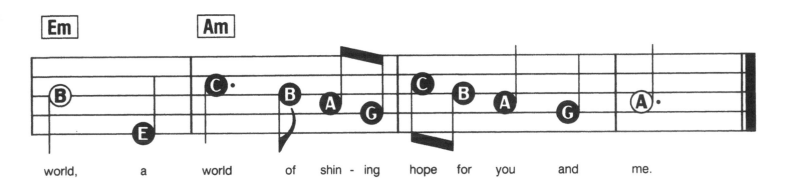

world,   a   world   of   shin - ing   hope   for   you   and   me.

Three Coins in the Fountain

from THREE COINS IN THE FOUNTAIN

Registration 2
Rhythm: Swing

Words by Sammy Cahn
Music by Jule Styne

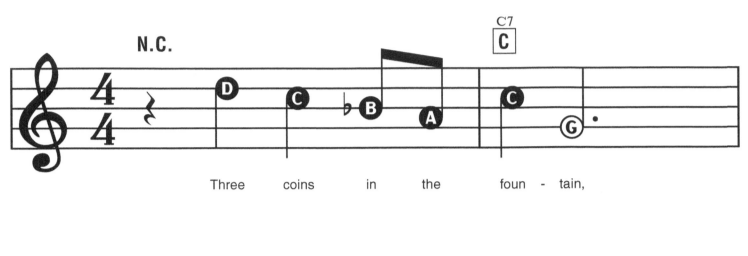

Three coins in the foun - tain,

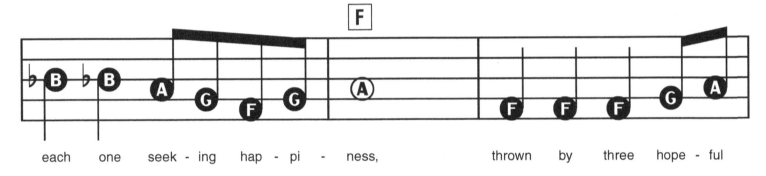

each one seek - ing hap - pi - ness, thrown by three hope - ful

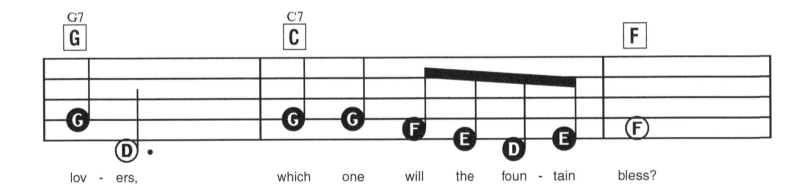

lov - ers, which one will the foun - tain bless?

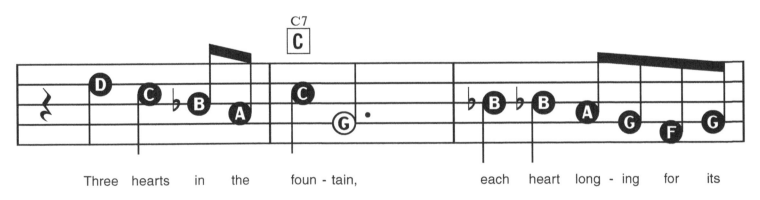

Three hearts in the foun - tain, each heart long - ing for its

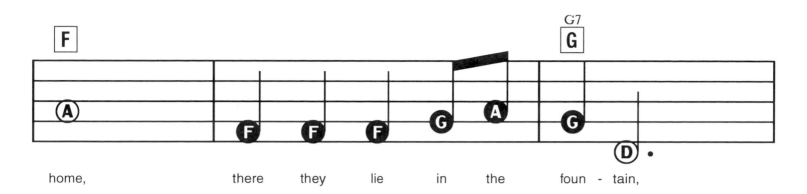

home, there they lie in the foun - tain,

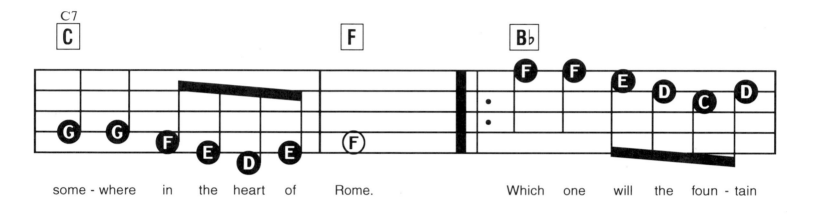

some - where in the heart of Rome. Which one will the foun - tain

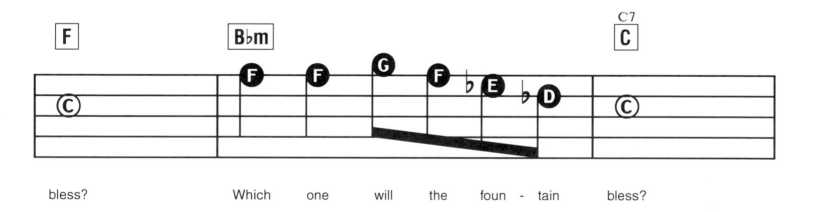

bless? Which one will the foun - tain bless?

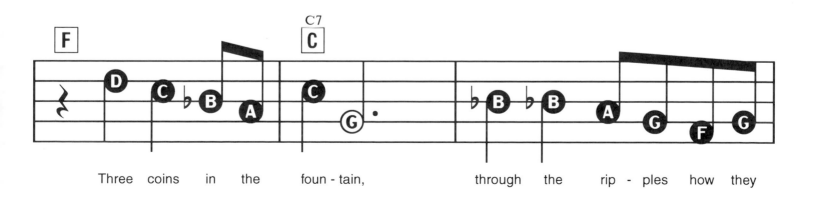

Three coins in the foun - tain, through the rip - ples how they

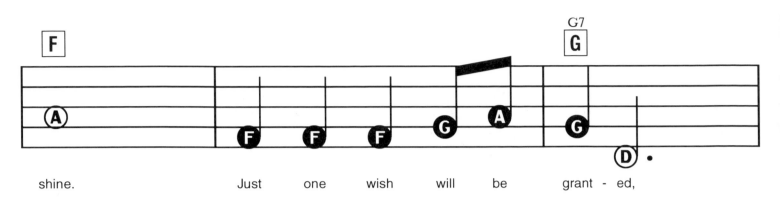

shine.   Just   one   wish   will   be   grant - ed,

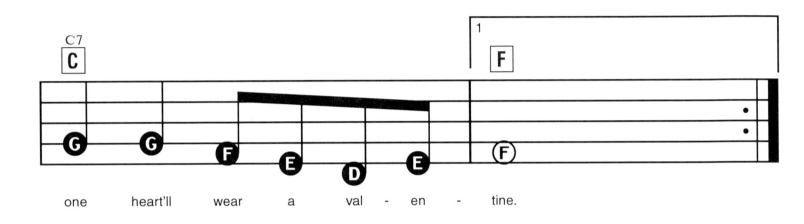

one   heart'll   wear   a   val - en - tine.

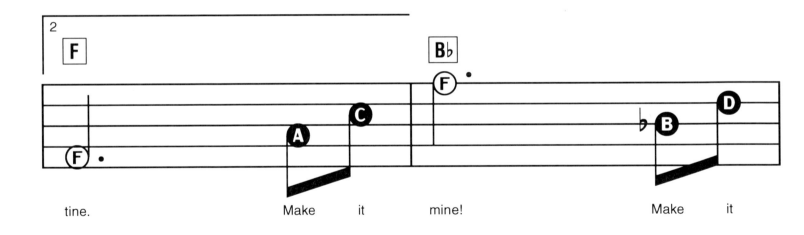

tine.   Make   it   mine!   Make   it

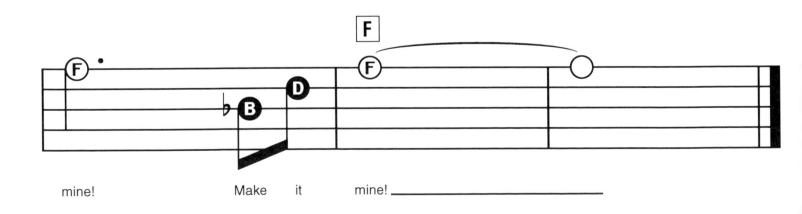

mine!   Make   it   mine! _____